HISTORY BENEATH YOUR FEET

THE AZTECS

PETER CHRISP

WAYLAND

History Beneath Your Feet

Titles in this series

Ancient Egypt
Ancient Greece
Ancient Rome
The Aztecs

Series editor: Alex Woolf
Development editor: Jonathan Ingoldby
Book editor: Liz Harman
Series design: Christopher Halls at Mind's Eye Design
Project artwork: John Yates
Production controller: Carol Stevens
Consultant: Professor Michael E Smith of the
Department of Anthropology at the University at
Albany, USA

First published 1999 by Wayland Publishers Ltd,
61 Western Road, Hove, East Sussex, BN3 1JD, England

Find Wayland on the Internet at
http://www.wayland.co.uk

Printed and bound in Italy by G. Canale & C.Sp.A.,
Turin

British Library Cataloguing in Publication Data
Chrisp, Peter
The Aztecs. - (History beneath your feet)
1.Aztecs - Juvenile literature
I.Title
972'.018

ISBN 0 7502 2363 4

The publishers would like to thank the following for
permission to publish their pictures:
AKG, London 14, 25, (Erich Lessing) 32 (right); Bodleian
Library, Oxford (Ms.Arch.Seld.A.1.4v) 24 (third–fifth),
(Ms.Arch.Seld.A.1.Fol.69r) 26 and 24 (second),
(Ms.Arch.Seld.A.1.Fol.60r) 30 (bottom) and 21 (first) and
31 (bottom); Bridgeman Art Library (British Museum,
London) 21, (Giraudon) 27 (top) and 44 (third); e t
archive 20, 29 (bottom) and 30 (top), 40; Michael Holford
title page and 8, 36 (both); Edward Parker 4 and 44 (first),
6; N J Saunders 10, 38, 42; Professor Michael E. Smith 23,
27 (bottom), 28, 29 (top), 43; South American Pictures
cover (main), (Robert Francis) 5 and 44 (second), 11 (top),
(Tony Morrison) 12, 16 (bottom), (Chris Sharp) 7;
Wayland Picture Library 11 (bottom) and 45 (right), 41,
(Biblioteca Laurenziana, Florence) 19 and 45 (left), 39;
(Biblioteca Nazionale Centrale, Florence) 16 (top), 22,
(British Museum, London) cover (small), title page, 35;
Werner Forman Archive (British Museum, London) 15, 31
(top), (Museum fur Volkerkunden, Basel) 34, (National
Museum of Anthropology, Mexico City) 9, 13, 18, 32
(left).

All Wayland books encourage children to read and help them improve their literacy.

 The contents page, page numbers, headings and index help locate specific pieces of information.

 The glossary reinforces alphabetic knowledge and extends vocabulary.

 The further information section suggests other books dealing with the same subject.

 Find out more about how this book is specifically relevant to the National Literacy Strategy on page 46.

CONTENTS

WHAT IS ARCHAEOLOGY?

'Archaeology' is a Greek word meaning 'the study of ancient things'. Archaeologists study the remains of people, buildings and objects from earlier times and then piece together what life had been like in the past. Some of these remains are so old that they have become hidden by earth or more recent buildings. This means that archaeologists first have to find where these remains are hidden, and then dig down or 'excavate' to see what is there. This is why so much history is 'beneath your feet'.

WHO WERE THE AZTECS?

Mexico City, the capital of Mexico, is the biggest and fastest-growing city in the Americas. It is a modern city of tall buildings and busy roads. More than eight million people live and work here.

Beneath the traffic that rushes through these streets, lie the ruins of an older, lost, city. It was called Tenochtitlan, which means 'cactus rock'. From the 1300s until the 1520s, Tenochtitlan was home to a people we call the Aztecs.

Beneath the huge, modern expanse of Mexico City lie the remains of the Aztec city of Tenochtitlan.

Tenochtitlan was an unusual city. It was built by the Aztecs on marshy islands in the middle of Lake Texcoco. Long causeways joined the city to the shore, where there were many other cities. Instead of streets, parts of Tenochtitlan were linked by canals and people travelled about by paddling wooden canoes.

THE AZTEC
EMPIRE 1519

0   100   200 miles
0   100   200   300 km.

GULF OF
MEXICO

Tula • • Teotihuacan
Tenochtitlan •

PACIFIC
OCEAN

A WARLIKE PEOPLE

Tenochtitlan was built on the lake for protection against attack. The cities on and around the lake were constantly at war with each other. War was fought partly for religious reasons. All the peoples of Mexico wanted to capture prisoners so that they could be sacrificed – killed as offerings to their gods.

THE NAME 'AZTEC'

The people of Tenochtitlan called themselves the *Mexica*, which is where the name Mexico comes from. We call them Aztec because they said they originally came from a place called Aztlan ('place of white herons').

The most successful fighters of all were the Aztecs of Tenochtitlan. In 1428, they joined forces with two neighbouring towns – Texcoco and Tlacopan. Led by the Aztecs, the armies of the three towns were able to conquer almost all their neighbours.

The Aztecs did not directly rule the peoples they conquered. Instead, the Aztecs forced people to give them tribute – food, precious stones, feathers and other valuable goods. The lands that paid tribute to the Aztecs are known as the Aztec Empire.

Tenayuca, north of Mexico City, was one of Tenochtitlan's neighbouring towns. There, an Aztec pyramid temple still stands, showing what temples at Tenochtitlan probably looked like.

BEFORE THE AZTECS

Long before the Aztecs, there were other civilizations (peoples) in Mexico. The most ancient civilization that we know about were the Olmecs, who lived from about 1200 BC to about 100 BC on the coast of the Gulf of Mexico.

North-east of Mexico City lie the ruins of a vast city which the Aztecs called Teotihuacan ('The Place of the Gods'). Radiocarbon dating has shown that the city flourished from around AD 150 until AD 650, when many of the buildings were burned. Although the Aztecs knew nothing about the people who built Teotihuacan, they worshipped similar gods. Teotihuacan has many statues and pictures of a rain god, called Tlaloc, who was also worshipped by the Aztecs.

The ruins of the huge city of Teotihuacan, which has wide, straight streets and pyramid temples.

THE TOLTECS

The oldest civilisation the Aztecs knew about was that of the Toltecs, which lasted from around AD 950 to 1150. The Aztecs told stories about the Toltecs, who they thought of almost as gods. They said that the Toltecs had invented every human skill, and that they were so clever that they could grow cotton already coloured red, yellow and blue. The Aztecs dug among the ruins of Tula, the Toltec city, and brought many of the treasures they found back to Tenochtitlan.

These enormous Toltec warriors once held up the roof of a temple at Tula.

Finds from Tula show that the Toltecs and the Aztecs had a lot in common. Both peoples were warlike, and both sacrificed their prisoners to the gods. At Tula, archaeologists dug up four pillars, carved to look like enormous warriors, each wearing a feather headdress (right). They had big butterflies carved on their chests. To the Toltecs and, later, the Aztecs, butterflies stood for the souls of dead warriors. After a warrior had died in battle or been sacrificed, his soul was thought to fly away like a butterfly.

LOOKING FOR TENOCHTITLAN

In the 1520s, the Aztec Empire was conquered by the Spaniards. The temples of Tenochtitlan were pulled down, and the statues of the gods were smashed. Over the ruins of the Aztec capital, the Spaniards built a new city, which we now know as Mexico City.

Until the 1970s, little archaeological work was done in Mexico City. Buildings, streets and underground pipes make it almost impossible to start digging in a city.

Over the years, several Aztec sculptures were discovered in Mexico City by accident. In 1790, some workmen laying pipes found a huge sculpture of the Aztec goddess Coatlicue ('Serpent Skirt'). At the time, people were so horrified by this statue, which looked like a devil, that they buried it again.

A terrifying statue of the goddess Coatlicue. She wears a skirt of rattlesnakes and her necklace is made of hands, hearts and a skull.

In February 1978, workers digging trenches unearthed a stone decorated with carvings. They called in archaeologists, who cleared away the earth to reveal a huge round stone. Carved on the surface was the figure of a woman, chopped into pieces. She was Coyolxauhqui, the Aztec moon goddess.

The fact that the carving was in such good condition was really exciting. The archaeologists knew from old maps that the Aztecs' main temple had stood right next to the spot where the stone was found. Perhaps the temple had not been totally destroyed by the Spaniards and was still waiting to be discovered!

BELLS ON HER CHEEKS

The stone carving of Coyolxauhqui found in 1978 illustrated an Aztec story. According to the story, Coyolxauhqui fought a fierce battle with her brother – the war and Sun god, Huitzilopochtli (Humming Bird) – on top of a mountain. He chopped up her body and threw it to the bottom of the mountain.

A huge stone carving of the head of the Aztec moon goddess, Coyolxauhqui.

The picture on the right shows another carving of Coyolxauhqui. There were three clues that helped archaeologists to identify her. Firstly, she has her eyes closed, which is a sign that she is dead. She also has bells carved on her cheeks and a moon-shaped nose ornament. The archaeologists knew the story of the Aztec moon goddess, Coyolxauhqui, who was murdered by her brother, and they knew that Coyolxauhqui means 'Bells on her Cheeks', so they guessed that this dead goddess was Coyolxauhqui.

THE GREAT TEMPLE

Following the discovery in 1978 of the carving of the Aztec goddess, Coyolxauqui, the Mexican Government decided to pay for a massive archaeological dig in the centre of Mexico City. In March 1978, the archaeologists, led by Eduardo Matos Moctezuma, began to look for the Great Temple of the Aztecs.

The excavation in 1983 of smaller temples that the Aztecs built close to the Great Temple.

There were several advantages to working in the middle of the capital city. Mexico City is home to many experts, who could be called in at short notice when their knowledge was needed. There were the city planners, who warned the archaeologists where the sewers lay. Demolition experts were called in to pull down three modern buildings. When animal bones were discovered, scientists from the university could identify them. There were also many local students, who volunteered to help in the digging.

Matos's team knew what they were looking for, because the Great Temple had been drawn and described by both Aztecs and Spaniards in the 1520s. It was a large pyramid with two flights of stairs going up the outside. At the top were two small shrines which held the statues of the most important Aztec gods: Tlaloc, the rain god, and Huitzilopochtli, god of war and the Sun.

Surviving Aztec pyramids, like this one, helped the archaeologists in Mexico City to understand what they were looking for.

HUITZILOPOCHTLI

In 1519, the Spanish soldier Bernal Diaz climbed up the steps of the Great Temple of the Aztecs. This is how he described the statue of the war and Sun god, Huitzilopochtli:

'He had a broad face and huge terrible eyes. And there were so many precious stones, so much gold, so many pearls stuck to him that his whole body was covered with them. He was wrapped with huge snakes made of gold, and he held a bow and arrows. The walls and floor of his shrine were so splashed and caked with blood that they were black.'

An Aztec painting of Huitzilopochtli, armed with a magic snake.

UNCOVERING THE TEMPLE

Although Matos Moctezuma's team knew what the Great Temple looked like, there was a surprise waiting for them. As they dug, they uncovered not one temple, but six, built on top of each other. There was a seventh temple, the oldest, but it was too deep to dig up. This shows that, as the Aztec Empire grew, the rulers rebuilt their temple, making it bigger and more impressive each time.

The Aztecs had carved the date of each rebuilding on the temple walls. The earliest building found was carved with the date '2 Rabbit', meaning 1390. The latest date was '1 Rabbit', or 1506, less than 20 years before the Spanish arrived.

STRATA

Archaeological sites often have different strata (layers). Usually, the oldest layers are found underneath more recent layers. Archaeologists have to tell one layer from another.

With the Great Temple, the layers are not on top of each other but side by side. This is because the Spaniards destroyed the top half of the building, letting us see the walls of several stages at once. The oldest temple sits in the middle, surrounded by the walls of later temples. The walls of the latest temple surround all the others.

This photograph shows the walls of the different stages of the Great Temple.

THE AZTEC CALENDAR

The Aztecs kept track of years with pictures and numbers. The years were numbered from one to 13 and each year was given one of four picture signs – a rabbit, a reed, a flint and a house.

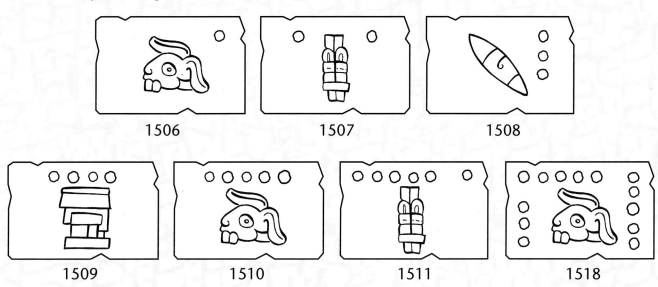

1506   1507   1508

1509   1510   1511   1518

After 13 Rabbit, the number went back to 1 Reed, 2 Flint, 3 House, and so on. It has been possible to work out what the dates mean because Aztec books show the coming of the Spaniards in 1519 as '1 Reed'.

In 1790, a huge carved stone was discovered. It has been called the 'calendar stone' because it is covered with Aztec dates. The stone shows the whole of history, as the Aztecs understood it. They believed that there had been four suns before our present one, each destroyed in turn. The carvings show how each sun was destroyed – by jaguars, hurricanes, fiery rain and a flood.

According to the Aztec 'calendar stone', our own sun will be destroyed by earthquakes.

PRESENTS FOR THE GODS

As the archaeologists dug deeper into the Great Temple, they uncovered more than a hundred collections of objects, including masks, jewellery and the bones of various animals. When they were building the temple, the Aztecs had placed these objects in stone containers behind the walls and under the floors. They must have been buried in the temple as presents for the gods.

Tlaloc, the rain god, was worshipped long before the time of the Aztecs. Nobody knows what his name means.

TLALOC THE RAIN GOD

Many of the offerings were linked with water. There were shells and carvings of shells, the bones of sea creatures such as sharks and stingrays and sea urchins, and models of frogs. These offerings were meant for the rain god, Tlaloc, and were often found with sculptures or masks of Tlaloc. He is easy to recognize because he has round goggle eyes and long teeth.

Tlaloc was one of the most important gods, because he was thought to bring the rain that made plants grow. The Aztecs believed that he had helpers, little Tlalocs, who carried jugs of water up into the sky during the rainy season. They smashed the jugs with sticks to release the rain. The sound of thunder during rain storms was believed to be the noise of the pots being smashed.

One collection of offerings found in the temple included the skeletons of more than 40 small children. According to Spanish and Aztec writings, children were killed every winter as sacrifices to Tlaloc. They were offered to the god so that he would provide rain in the coming year.

This stone carving shows one of Tlaloc's helpers releasing rain from a jug.

BIOLOGISTS

One of the greatest challenges of the dig was identifying the large number of animal bones and other remains that were found. A team of biologists worked with the archaeologists, examining all the bones. Sometimes, they had only one bone to work with, but they were still able to say what animal it came from. They identified the bones of big cats such as jaguars and pumas and birds such as toucans and eagles, as well as crocodiles, wolves, turtles, snakes and many types of fish.

HUMAN SACRIFICE

The Great Temple was a place for human sacrifice. Prisoners captured in battle were led up the steps to the platform at the top. Here, the prisoners were stretched out on their backs over a stone block. Then an Aztec priest cut out their hearts with a stone knife. The hearts were burned as offerings to Huitzilopochtli, god of war and the Sun, and the bodies were thrown down the steps.

An Aztec painting of a human sacrifice at the Great Temple.

Matos Moctezuma's team uncovered the platform of one of the oldest levels of the temple. Here, in front of the shrine of the war god, they found the stone block used in the sacrifices.

Carvings of skulls decorating the stone base of the skull rack.

Among the offerings buried in the temple, the archaeologists found the skulls of men who had been sacrificed. Holes had been drilled through the skulls so they could be displayed on poles on a skull rack, a platform near the temple. According to a Spaniard who saw the skull rack, there were so many skulls that 'they were impossible to count, so close together that they caused fright and wonder'.

PROJECT: A MODEL OF THE GREAT TEMPLE

You will need:
White or pale brown card
A ruler
Scissors
Glue
Corrugated paper
Red and blue paint

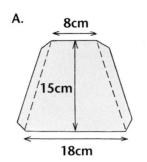

A. 8cm / 15cm / 18cm

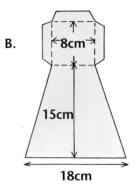

B. 8cm / 15cm / 18cm

1. Cut out three pieces of white card like shape A (above) and one like shape B.

2. Fold along the dotted lines and glue the tabs together.

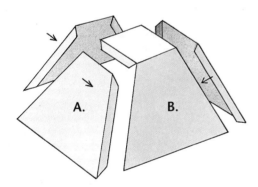

3. To make the steps, cut two strips of corrugated paper and stick them to the front of the pyramid. Put some red paint on the steps, to look like blood-stains.

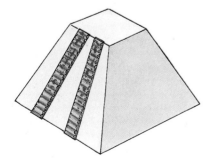

4. On white card, draw and cut out two shapes like shape C (below). Fold and stick them to make the gods' shrines.

5. Tlaloc's shrine should be painted with blue stripes to stand for falling rain. Draw skulls on Huitzilopochtli's shrine to stand for sacrificed warriors.

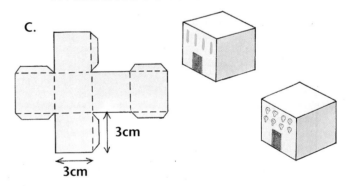

C. 3cm / 3cm

6. Stick the shrines on top of the temple.

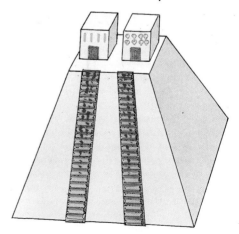

WARRIORS

Just to the north of the Great Temple, the archaeologists found a buried building. In the doorway, there were two life-sized pottery statues of men, dressed as eagles. The statues had wings, claws and beaked helmets. Their arms were stretched out, as if they were about to flap their wings and take off.

The archaeologists recognised the pottery statues from Aztec books. They were Eagle Warriors, a special group of Aztec fighters who went into battle dressed as eagles. The Eagle Warriors were the servants of the Sun. Their role was to capture prisoners in battle. They brought the prisoners to the temple to sacrifice them to Huitzilopochtli, god of war and the Sun. By feeding the god with human hearts, the Eagle Warriors believed that they gave the Sun the strength to shine each day.

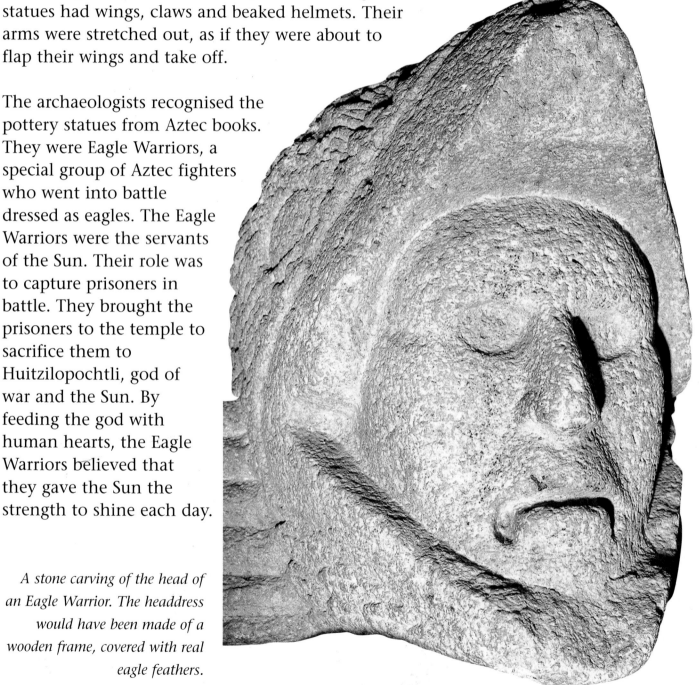

A stone carving of the head of an Eagle Warrior. The headdress would have been made of a wooden frame, covered with real eagle feathers.

A second group of Aztec warriors dressed in jaguar skins and were called Jaguar Warriors. The jaguar was the most powerful and feared hunter in the forests of Central America. Hunting by night, this big cat was linked with the god of the night sky, Tezcatlipoca (Smoking Mirror). Jaguar Warriors were special servants of Tezcatilpoca.

An Aztec warrior was armed with a wooden sword-club called a *maquahuitl*. It was set with blades made from a type of stone called obsidian. The blade was so sharp that it could cut off a man's head with one blow. But the Aztecs did not want to kill their enemies in battle. It was more important to wound them so that they could be captured.

Aztec men won respect and privileges by capturing prisoners. A warrior who captured one prisoner was allowed to wear special face-paint. If he captured four, he could wear lip plugs and a headdress of eagle feathers. The most successful of all could become Eagle Warriors.

An Aztec painting of a Jaguar Warrior, armed with a maqahuitl *sword-club.*

Aztec warriors going into battle.

Thanks to Aztec pictures such as this, archaeologists were able to recognize that the pottery figures found at the Great Temple were Eagle Warriors.

TRIBUTE

Capturing prisoners for sacrifice was not the only reason for going to war. Just as important was the need to conquer other peoples, to force them to pay tribute, in the form of food, clothing and precious goods. There were around 200,000 Aztecs living in Tenochtitlan, and the area around their city could not supply all they needed. The Aztecs had to have the tribute to live.

We know a lot about the tribute that was paid because of a beautiful book called the *Codex Mendoza*. This is a book all about the Aztec Empire, painted by Aztec artists for their new Spanish rulers. In pictures, the book shows the tribute paid by 371 other towns.

The page from the codex that you can see on page 21 shows the tribute paid by seven towns on the Gulf of Mexico. Their names are shown in pictures on the left. One town was called Tuchpa, which means 'on the rabbit'. It is shown at the top left by a picture of a rabbit.

An Aztec drawing of weeping prisoners in a cage.

FINDS OF TRIBUTE

When they were digging up the Great Temple, the archaeologists found that most of the offerings buried there were not from Tenochtitlan. The bones of jaguars, for example, must have come from the jungles to the south. The sharks and sea-shells could only have come from the coasts to the north and south. These must have come to Tenochtitlan as trade, or as tribute.

The pictures on the right of the codex page below show the goods paid to the Aztecs every six months. Can you see the two big bags on the right of the picture? On top of each there is a picture of a chilli pepper and a feather. A feather stood for the number 400, so every six months, these towns had to send 800 bags of chilli peppers to Tenochtitlan as tribute.

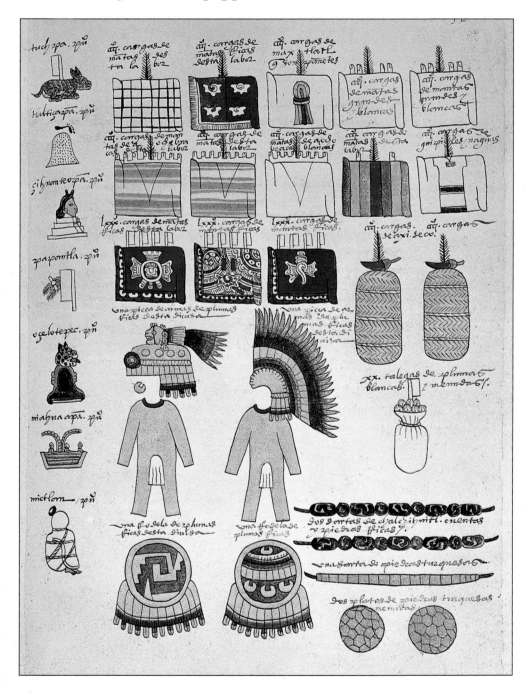

Tribute items, including colourful cloaks, chilli peppers, warriors' costumes, shields, bags of white feathers and various beads.

DEATH AND BURIAL

The Aztecs had various ways of burying the dead. According to a Spanish friar, Diego Duran, 'Some people were buried in the fields, others in the courtyards of their own homes. Others were burned and their ashes buried in temples.'

In the 1980s, the archaeologist, Professor Michael E. Smith, found the skeletons of 14 children when he was digging up Aztec houses (see page 29). The children had all been buried beneath the floors or in the yards of the houses. The children were buried in a sitting position, with their knees pulled up to their chests. Aztec pictures often show dead people in this position, wrapped up in a bundle of cloth.

This Aztec picture shows a merchant's funeral. He sits, wrapped in a bundle, surrounded by his most precious belongings.

It is a mystery why the Aztecs chose to bury the children in their houses. Professor Smith suggests that the children were still thought of as part of the family, so they belonged at home with the living family members. Today in Mexico, there is a festival called the Day of the Dead, when people pay their respects to their dead relatives. They visit family graves, take their dead relatives food and flowers, and talk to them. Perhaps the Aztecs remembered their own dead children with similar customs at home.

A child's body dug up by the archaeologist Michael E. Smith. You can see the skull, and the arms wrapped around the knees.

OSTEOLOGY

Osteology, the study of bones, can give us lots of information about the dead. The size and shape of bones tells us the age and sex of the dead person. The state of bones can be evidence of disease or of a poor diet or even how a person died. A bad diet often causes light, brittle bones. Bones that have broken at some point, but healed well, are a sign of good health.

Compared with Europeans of the same period, the Aztecs were very healthy. Diseases that were common in Europe, such as measles, influenza, typhoid and tuberculosis, were unknown in America. Unfortunately, the Spaniards brought these diseases with them when they conquered Mexico and many Aztecs died as a result.

WRITTEN EVIDENCE

The Aztecs created painted books, called codices. These were drawn using dyes made from soot and plants on sheets of folded deerskin or paper made from bark. The subjects of the codices included Aztec history, their calendar, and religious rituals, such as sacrifice. Codices also listed the tribute owed to the Aztecs by the cities of their empire.

The Aztecs used pictures instead of words.

A scroll beside a person's mouth showed that they were talking.

Footprints represented a journey.

A shield and arrows stood for war.

A burning temple stood for a victory in battle.

Because Tenochtitlan means 'cactus rock', its symbol was a picture of a cactus on a rock.

The Aztec ruler, Chimalpopoca (Smoking Shield) was pictured with his name sign above his head (smoke rising from a shield).

SPANISH WRITERS

Some of what we know about Aztec life comes from the books and letters of several Spaniards who wrote at the time of the Spanish conquest. After the conquest, many Spanish friars travelled to Mexico to spread their faith. To make their job easier, some learned the Aztec language, *nahuatl*, and found out about Aztec beliefs. Two Spanish friars, Diego Duran and Bernardino de Sahagun, wrote books filled with the stories and memories of old Aztec men. Duran wrote a history of the Aztec Empire and Sahagun described Aztec religious festivals and daily life. Both friars used Aztec artists to illustrate their books.

Thanks to all these written records, we know more about the Aztecs that we do about almost any other American people who lived before the arrival of the Europeans. This was a great help to archaeologists studying the Aztecs. For example, before they started to dig for Aztec temples, they knew from the writings what these might look like. When they found a statue of a god, they knew which god it was thanks to descriptions and pictures in Aztec books.

This is the earliest Spanish map of Teotihuacan.

PALACES

Apart from the Great Temple, the biggest buildings in Tenochtitlan were the palaces of the Aztec rulers. There were at least four palaces, each built by a different *tlatoani*, or ruler. The palaces were enormous buildings with hundreds of rooms, including libraries, storerooms and workshops. One Spaniard wrote that he walked through an Aztec palace until his legs could carry him no further, and he still hadn't seen everything.

The palace was the home of the ruler, and the centre of government. The Aztec drawing on the right shows the palace of Moctezuma II, the ruler of the empire from 1502–20. He is sitting at the top, in his throne room. On either side, there are guest houses where the great lords of the empire stayed when they were visiting Moctezuma. On the bottom left, you can see the hall where the Aztec war leaders met. On the right, four judges try cases.

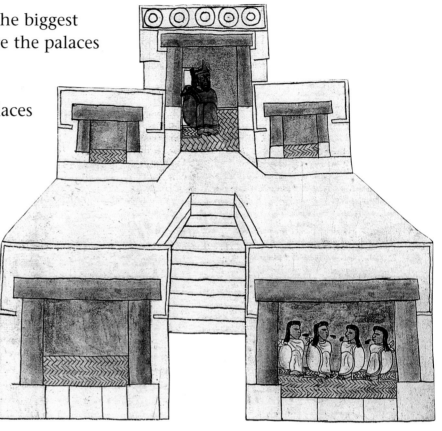

Moctezuma's palace was much bigger than this Aztec drawing suggests.

MOCTEZUMA'S BIRD HOUSE

Moctezuma's palace included gardens and a private zoo, described by the Spaniard, Hernan Cortes:

'There were ten pools in which were kept all kinds of water birds. For the sea birds, there were pools of salt water, and there was fresh water for the river birds. Above the pools were balconies, finely made, where Moctezuma came to amuse himself by watching the birds.'

This Aztec picture shows the crowning of the emperor Moctezuma, in 1502.

EXCAVATING PALACES

The palaces of Tenochtitlan are still waiting to be found by archaeologists. However, several smaller palaces have been discovered in other towns of the Aztec Empire. One of the best was found in 1989, under a big mound at Yautepec, 50 km south of Mexico City. The archaeologists could tell that it was a palace because of its size – 6,000 m^2 – and because it was raised up on a high platform. Unlike ordinary houses, its walls were made of stone rather than mud bricks, and they were painted in different colours.

This Aztec palace at Yautepec is the first to have been excavated by archaeologists. So far, only about a quarter of this enormous palace has been uncovered.

HOUSES

Like many Mexicans today, ordinary Aztecs lived in houses built of sun-dried mud brick with thatched roofs. Over time, mud bricks crumble into dust, leaving nothing behind for archaeologists to find. Luckily, the Aztecs laid their bricks on a low stone foundation wall, and they lined their floors with stone. In many places, you can still find the stone foundations of Aztec houses.

These Mexican children live in a thatched, mud-brick house, built in the same way as the houses of their Aztec ancestors.

GEOPHYSICS

Archaeologists have several ways of finding buried stone walls. They can 'look below' the surface of the ground with geophysics (earth sciences). One method uses resistivity – an electrical current is passed into the earth, and the amount of resistance to it is measured. Buried walls have a high resistance. Geophysicists walk over an area with electrical probes, and then use a computer to turn their findings into a plan of the site.

Archaeologists uncover the stone foundation walls of Aztec houses.

CUEXCOMATE AND CAPILCO

In 1985–86, the archaeologist Professor Michael E. Smith studied 42 ordinary Aztec houses in the town of Cuexcomate and a nearby village, Capilco. He did not need to use geophysics to find the houses, because the foundation walls were not deeply buried and could still be seen.

Smith found that the houses were tiny, with only one room. Often, two to five houses were arranged around a shared courtyard. The small size of the houses suggests that much of the household work was done in the open air, in the courtyard. The Aztecs had a word for a group of families living closely together. It is *cemithualtin*, which means 'those in one yard'.

Mostly, it was the women who worked together in the yard, preparing meals and spinning and weaving cotton. The men spent much of their time away from home, working in the fields.

An Aztec couple sit outside their house on a reed mat.

AZTEC RUBBISH

Each Aztec house had its own midden (rubbish heap). An ancient rubbish heap is one of the best places for an archaeologist to dig. You can learn a lot about people's lives from the things they throw away.

Aztec rubbish contains hardly any animal bones, so we know that ordinary people did not eat very much meat. The few bones that were found show that the Aztecs sometimes ate fish, deer, rabbit, iguana (a sort of lizard), turkey, duck and dog. We know that they mostly lived on maize and beans, which they ate at every meal.

All Aztec meals were cooked by women, over an open fire.

Stone grinding tools were a common find. Women used these to grind maize into flour. Smith also found broken pottery griddles (hotplates), on which the women baked flat maize loaves, called *tortillas*, which are still an important part of the Mexican diet.

POTTERY STYLES

The commonest find in Aztec rubbish is broken pottery. Pottery is a useful find because its style has changed over time. Archaeologists learn to recognise different pottery styles, and can work out roughly when pots were made. Dating the pottery in rubbish heaps helps them to find out when people were living in the houses.

An Aztec drawing of a woman teaching her daughter to grind corn for making tortillas.

Only a quarter of the houses that Michael Smith studied in Capilco had pottery made in early Aztec times (before 1350). But all the houses had later Aztec pottery, dating from after 1440. This shows that the population was growing – as time went on, more houses were built.

Both the shape and decoration of Aztec pottery are clues, helping archaeologists to date pots.

An Aztec mother teaches her daughter to use a loom to weave spun cotton into cloth.

SPINNING COTTON

Aztec mothers taught their daughters to spin cotton using a weighted stick, called a spindle. A woman would rest the spindle in a little bowl, to help her to control the twirling spindle. Michael Smith discovered pottery spindle weights in almost every rubbish heap. He also found small bowls which had been used for spinning. He could tell this because the bowls had traces of rubbing, caused by the spindles, on their inner surfaces.

CRAFTS

Otumba, in the Teotihuacan valley, was an important town in Aztec times. Over time, all the Aztec buildings have been destroyed. But if you walk across the fields, you can find small pieces of pottery and other Aztec objects lying on the ground.

In the late 1980s, there was a project to map Otumba using a technique called field walking. Archaeologists drew a map on which they divided the whole area into a grid, made up of 1,150 squares of 5 m by 5 m. Volunteers were each given a square on the grid, which they had to walk over slowly, looking out for Aztec finds. Every find was marked in its place on the map. Field walking allowed the archaeologists to draw a map of a lost Aztec town. When they stopped finding Aztec objects, they had reached the edge of the town.

The finds showed that Otumba was a craft centre, where various products were made, including pottery, cloth, stone tools and jewellery.

FEATHERWORKING

This headdress is one of the few surviving examples of the Aztec craft of featherworking. Coloured feathers were used to make pictures on shields, cloaks and headdresses. According to the early Spanish writer, Sahagun, this was a family business. Men did the designs and applied the feathers. The women dyed the feathers, while the children made the glue.

Aztec craft workers made beautiful gold jewellery. It is rarely found by archaeologists, as most Aztec gold was melted down by the Spanish.

PROJECT: A FEATHER HEADDRESS

You will need:
Black card, green card, blue card
Gold paper or foil
Scissors
Glue
A stapler

1. Cut a strip of black card to make a headband this shape, 20 cm by 60 cm.

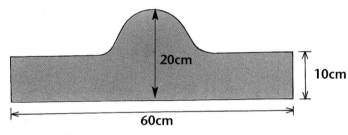

20cm

10cm

60cm

2. Wrap the headband round your head and mark where the ends meet. Take it off and staple the overlapping ends together.

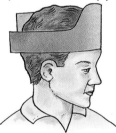

3. Cut the green card into lots of feather-shaped pieces about 35 cm long. Make six longer feathers, about 45 cm long. You can cut slits along each side to make them look more like feathers.

4. Glue the feathers to the front of the headband. Stick the long feathers upright in the middle.

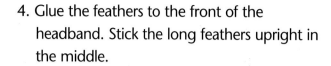
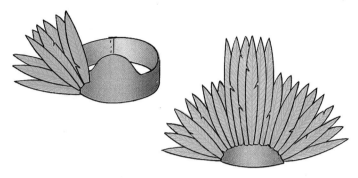

5. Cut the blue card into a semi-circle 10 cm wide and glue it over the front of the headdress.

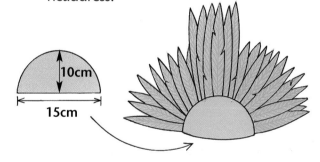

10cm

15cm

6. Cut the gold paper into little circles and half-moon shapes and glue them onto the blue card.

STONEWORKERS

At Otumba, archaeologists found thousands of pieces of obsidian, a glassy black rock that was used to make jewellery, tools and weapons. Every Aztec family needed obsidian blades, for knives and other tools. Obsidian has the sharpest edge of any known tool, but it is easily broken. People threw away their broken blades, so pieces of obsidian are among the commonest finds on any Aztec site.

It took amazing skill to make this mask from obsidian. The obsidian had to be chipped into shape, using stone tools, then ground and polished, using sand and cloths.

DATING OBSIDIAN

Obsidian is a useful find because it can be dated. As soon as a blade is made, it starts to take in water from its surroundings. This forms a tiny 'rind' or layer on the surface of the blade. The thicker the rind is, the older the blade is. Using a powerful microscope, scientists can measure the thickness of the rind, then work out how long ago a blade was made.

MAKING OBSIDIAN BLADES

To find out how things were made in the past, archaeologists do experiments, trying different ways of making the object using the materials that would have been available. Archaeologist John Clark, has spent years trying different ways to find out how the Aztecs made their obsidian blades.

Clark found that the Aztecs probably sat down to work, holding the obsidian between their feet, and leaning forward, pressing on the stone with a tool held against their chests. First, the craftsman made a cylinder-shaped blade 'core' with a stone tool. Then, a pointed wooden or bone tool was pressed against the top edge of the core until a sharp piece split off. This was the blade. Using this method, a skilled worker could make 150–200 blades from a single core in a short time.

STONE TOOLS

Other craftsmen made tools from different kinds of stone, especially flint which is much harder than obsidian. Flint was used to make most of the knife blades used in human sacrifice. Flint had a special importance to the Aztecs. It was one of the symbols used as the name of a day and year in the Aztec calendar. Flint knives, decorated to look like faces, were found at the Great Temple site. Flint was also useful because it could be struck to make sparks. Aztec families always used flints to light their fires.

This knife, with an Eagle Warrior on its handle, was used in human sacrifices.

TURQUOISE MASKS

One of the most precious Aztec craft materials was turquoise, a scarce stone of bright pale blue. Turquoise was cut into tiny tiles and used to decorate masks that were used in religious ceremonies. Aztec priests sometimes dressed up as the gods and wore masks showing the gods' faces.

The two masks shown on this page are among the best Aztec masks. They are in the British Museum, in London. The masks were not dug up by archaeologists. They come from the private collection of a rich Englishman, called Henry Christy.

A turquoise mask of the fire god, Xiuhtecuhtli (Turquoise Lord). The teeth and eyes are made of sea-shells.

In the late 1800s, he bought many Aztec works of art which had been taken to Europe.

Nobody knows how the masks ended up in Europe. They may have been part of a gift from the Aztecs to the Spanish leader, Hernan Cortes. When the Spaniards first arrived in Mexico, the Aztecs did not know if they were men or gods. They had never seen ships before, or men in armour.

This mask of the god of the night sky, Tezcatlipoca (Smoking Mirror), is made from the skull of a victim of human sacrifice.

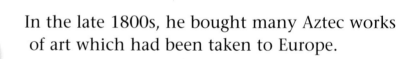

PROJECT: A MASK OF THE FIRE GOD

You will need:
Black card and white card
Scissors
Glue
Pale blue paper

1. Cut a piece of black card into a face shape, with holes for the eyes and nose.

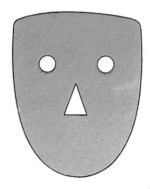

2. Cut a piece of black card to make the nose. Bend the nose and push the tabs at the sides into the nose hole and stick them inside the mask.

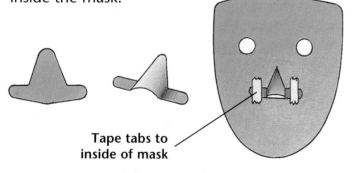

Tape tabs to inside of mask

3. Cut out white teeth and eye shapes. Make a hole in the centre of each eye. Stick the eyes and teeth onto the mask.

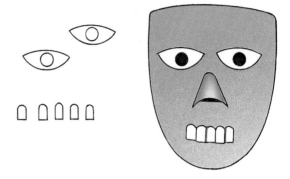

4. Cut out lots of tiny squares of blue paper and stick them all over the mask.

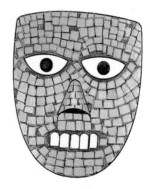

Emperor Moctezuma sent a great treasure to Cortes, hoping to please him. Cortes sent the treasure back to Europe. Moctezuma may have sent these masks to Cortes to find out which god he was. If he put on the turquoise mask, Moctezuma would have known that Cortes was the fire god.

FARMING

Around the marshy edges of Lake Texcoco, which surrounded the city of Tenochtitlan, the Aztecs grew their crops on small raised fields called *chinampas*. They built the *chinampas* by digging ditches, to take away the water. Then they drove wooden stakes into the earth, making a frame, into which they could pile mud, scooped from the lake-bed. *Chinampas* were very successful and produced several crops each year.

Lake Texcoco has mostly been drained now, to provide building land for Mexico City. However, there are a few lake areas where *chinampas* are still used today. Mexican farmers still paddle to their fields in flat-bottomed canoes, just like the Aztecs.

These chinampas, *built by Aztec farmers, are still in use today.*

On the hilly land around the lake different farming methods were used. In many places, you can still see stone walls built by Aztec farmers on the slopes of the hills. They piled soil behind the walls to make terraces – flat steps in the hillside. Like *chinampas*, some Aztec terraces are still used today.

A third farming method has been discovered by archaeologists. At Cuexcomate, Michael Smith found that the Aztecs had built stone walls, called check dams, across the beds of the local streams. The wall slowed down the flow of the stream, and trapped silt. The silt built up behind the wall to make an area for planting crops. When the silt reached the top, the wall had to be made higher. The Cuexcomate check dams were 2 m high, so must have been used for many years.

An Aztec farmer sowing, weeding and harvesting a crop of maize.

POLLEN

Archaeologists have many ways of finding out how land was used by farmers in the past. To learn which crops were grown, they look through the soil for ancient pollen. Each species of plant has a different shaped pollen grain, which can be identified using a microscope.

PRESERVING THE PAST

As soon as an ancient object is dug out of the earth, it needs to be protected. The digging up of the Great Temple was the start of a much bigger job – restoring and preserving the remains. Broken pottery had to be pieced together. Crumbling stonework and flaking paint was treated to stop further decay. A team of restorers worked in a laboratory on the site.

The Mexican government paid for the building of a big museum next to the temple, to display all the sculptures and other offerings that were found. Now you can visit the museum, and then walk all round the temple ruins. The Templo Mayor (Great Temple) Museum, as it is called, is one of the most popular tourist sites in Mexico.

The Great Temple site as it is today, with the modern museum behind.

One problem that will affect the Great Temple in the future is pollution. Mexico City has some of the worst traffic pollution in the world. The pollution causes acid rain, which eats away at stonework.

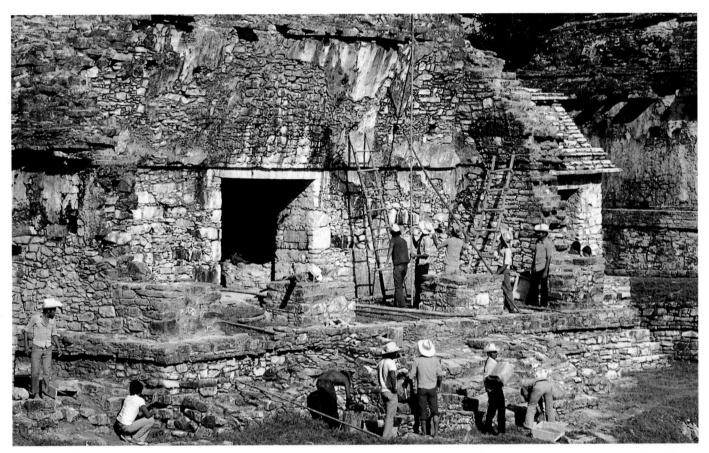

As well as Aztec remains, Mexico has many other important archaeological sites that need to be preserved. The stone of this building, built by the Maya, another ancient civilization, has worn away and is being preserved.

LOOTING

The worst enemy of Mexican archaeology is the looting (robbing) of archaeological sites. There are still many rich private collectors, who are willing to pay large amounts of money for ancient Mexican art. To find the treasures, looters break into tombs (burial chambers), taking away mosaic masks, painted pottery and jade carvings to sell. Teotihuacan and other sites are still being robbed today.

Archaeological finds are like pieces in a jigsaw puzzle. To see the whole picture, you need as many pieces as possible. For example, if you find a stone mask in a tomb, you can date it using the bones of the person buried with it. You can find out what sort of person was buried by other objects placed in the tomb. But looters would only be interested in the mask, because it is the only thing they could sell.

WHAT NEXT?

'A builder once told me how he dug up an Aztec war canoe. Rather than face the delays of an archaeological study, he told me, "I just paved over the whole thing." We can only guess at the number of other treasures still lying beneath the concrete.' (Eduardo Matos Moctezuma, Mexican archaeologist)

Most of ancient Tenochtitlan still lies buried beneath the streets of Mexico City. It is only when major building work takes place that Aztec ruins are discovered. Many more Aztec buildings are still waiting to be found. Archaeologists hope to discover the palaces of the rulers, the houses of the poor, the great market places. They also hope to find an Aztec ballcourt,

The temple of Ehecatl, the wind god, which was found in 1967 when tunnels were dug for Mexico City's underground railway.

a stone court where people played *tlachtli* a game with a rubber ball. It was usually played for religious reasons, with players taking on the roles of gods. The results of a game were used to tell the future.

Modern archaeology is about much more than digging up grand buildings, such as temples. Mexican archaeologists today spend much of their time working in the countryside, field walking, or sifting through Aztec rubbish heaps. Thanks to their work, we are still finding out more and more about the lives of ordinary Aztecs.

Archaeologists excavating Aztec burials at Yautepec, in the Mexican countryside. Digging here is much easier for archaeologists than digging in the city.

THE WATER PROBLEM

One problem facing archaeologists in Mexico is that the city was built on a lake. If you dig just a few metres down, you reach water. In order to dig in the lower, oldest, levels, you have to pump the water out. But if you do this, you risk damaging surrounding buildings. Archaeologists need to find new ways of controlling water before they can get down to the oldest levels of Tenochtitlan. This problem is also good news for archaeology. Water can be a preservative. Wood and other materials which quickly rot in dry soil can last for hundreds of years in water. So wooden buildings and canoes may still be found in the lower levels.

TIMELINES

AZTEC TIMELINE (ALL DATES ARE AD)

150–650	950–1150	about 1250	about 1325
Teotihuacan grows into a huge city (see page 4)	The Toltecs of Tula become the most powerful Mexican people (see page 7)	Aztecs arrive in the valley of Mexico	Aztecs build the city of Tenochtitlan on islands on Lake Texcoco (see page 4)

1428–40	1440–60	1486–1502	1502–20
Led by the Aztec emperor, Itzcoatl, the three towns conquer the valley of Mexico	Emperor Moctezuma I reigns, conquering more lands and rebuilding the Great Temple	Emperor Ahuitzotl conquers the southern coast of Mexico	The reign of Moctezuma II; the Aztec Empire reaches its largest size (see page 27)

ARCHAEOLOGICAL TIMELINE

1790	1910	1940	1940–46	1957–63	1967
Workmen digging in Mexico City discover the statue of the Aztec goddess, Coatlicue (see page 8)	Archaeologists discover many Aztec offerings buried near the Great Temple site	Mexican archaeologists, led by Jorge Acosta, excavate the Toltec city of Tula	Matthew Stirling digs at La Venta, a centre of the earliest known Mexican people, the Olmecs	René Millon finds out more about Teotihuacan by taking aerial photographs (photographs taken from above)	When building Mexico's underground railway system, workers uncover a temple of Ehecatl, the Aztec god of the wind (see page 42)

1391–1415	1428
Under the rule of King Huitzilihuitl the Aztecs become powerful soldiers	Aztecs join forces with two nearby cities – Texcoco and Tlacopan (see page 5)

1519	1521
The Spaniards arrive in Mexico	The Aztecs of Tenochtitlan surrender (give themselves up) to the Spanish (see page 8)

1978–82	1982	1985–86	1988–94	1989–96
Eduardo Matos Moctezuma leads a team of archaeologists who uncover the Aztec Great Temple in Mexico City (see page 10)	The experimental archaeologist, John Clark, publishes his findings about how Aztecs may have made obsidian blades (see page 35)	Michael Smith excavates Aztec houses at Cuexcomate and Capilco (see page 29)	Thomas Charlton, Cynthia Otis Charlton and Deborah Nichols use field-walking to map Otumba, an Aztec craft centre	Hortensia de Vega Nova excavates an Aztec palace at Yautepec (see page 27)

GLOSSARY

acid rain rain that can damage plants and buildings. This is because it contains acid, which comes from air pollution caused by cars and factories.

biologists scientists who study plants and animals.

canals waterways built by human beings.

causeways raised roadways, built to cross low or wet ground or an area of water.

courtyard an outdoor area enclosed by walls or buildings.

current flow of electricity.

demolition the pulling down of a building.

empire a group of states or countries controlled by one person or group of people.

excavating digging up.

foundation a solid base under a building.

friar A Roman Catholic holy man who tried to spread Christianity. Some friars were also priests, which meant that they could carry out religious ceremonies.

lip plugs items of jewellery worn in pierced lower lips.

mosaic a pattern made up from many small pieces of coloured glass or stone.

pyramid A building with sloping sides and, usually, a square base. The sides are usually triangular, but Aztec pyramids did not have triangular sides, as they had flat tops on which temples were built.

radiocarbon dating A scientific method of finding the date of ancient plant and animal remains.

sewers pipes or tunnels that carry away waste matter and water.

shrine a holy place with special religious importance.

silt tiny stones, soil and other matter that are carried in rivers and streams.

thatched with a covering of reeds or straw.

PRONUNCIATION GUIDE

Ahuitzotl – say 'ah-weet-zotl'
Ayotlan – say 'ah-yot-lan'
Cemithualtin – say 'sem-mit-wahl-tin'
Coatlicue – say 'co-at-lee-kway'
Coyolxauhqui – say 'coy-yol-shaow-kee'
Cuexcomate – say 'kwesh-co-ma-tay'
Huitzilihuitl – say 'weet-zee-lee-weetl'
Huitzilopochtli – say 'weet-zil-oh-poch-tlee'
Itzcoatl – say 'eetz-co-atl'
maquhuitl – say 'ma-ka-weet-il'
nahuatl – say 'nah-wah-tl'
Tenochtitlan – say 'tay-notch-tit-lan'

Teotihuacan – say 'tay-o-tee-wah-kan'
Texcoco – say 'tesh-co-co'
Tezcatlipoca – say 'tez-cat-lee-poh-ka'
tlachtli – say 'tlatch-tlee'
tlatoani – say 'tlah-toe-ah-nee'
Xiuhtecuhtli – say 'shee-oo-tee-coot-lee'

The following words are pronounced as they are written:

Aztlan, Calpolli, Capilco, chacmool, Chimalpopoca, chinampas, Moctezuma, Tenayuca, Tlacopan, Tlaloc

FURTHER INFORMATION

PLACES TO VISIT

The British Museum, London

The Museum of Mankind, Burlington Gardens, London

The Pitt Rivers Museum, Parks Road, Oxford

BOOKS

Aztecs
(The Ancient World series)
Robert Hull
(Wayland, 1997)

Food and Feasts with the Aztecs
Imogen Dawson
(Wayland, 1995)

If you were there in Aztec Times
Antony Mason
(Marshall Publishing, 1997)

WEBSITES

The Templo Mayor Museum in Mexico City:
http://archaeology.la.asu.edu/vm/mesoam/tm/pages2/index2.htm

This site has information about the Aztecs and pictures of some finds from the dig.

Teotihuacan:
http://archaeology.la.asu.edu/vm/mesoam/teo

This website has maps, pictures and film of discoveries made inside one of the pyramid temples

CD ROM

Ancient Lands (Microsoft)

CLUBS

The Young Archaeologist's Club
Bowes Morrell House
111 Walmgate
York YO1 2UA
Tel. 01904 671 417

Use this book for teaching literacy

This book can help you in the literacy hour in the following ways:

 Children can read and evaluate the projects in this book for their purpose, organisation and clarity. (Year 5, Term 1: Non-fiction reading comprehension)

 They can use this book to collect, define and spell technical words used by archaeologists or historians. (Year 5, Term 2: Vocabulary extension)

 The book is an example of an explanatory text in which children can investigate and note features of impersonal style. (Year 5, Term 2: Non-fiction reading comprehension)

 The discussion contained in chapters 12 and 13 can be used by children to draft and write letters of their own arguing the case for preserving the past for future generations. (Year 5, Term 3: Non-fiction writing composition)

INDEX

3/00

Please return/renew this item by the last date shown.

 BATH & NORTH EAST SOMERSET